THE Views at pages 31, 39, and 40, represent the improvements and restorations already effected, and intended to be so, when completed. Towards this laudable object the Public are respectfully invited to contribute. The application of the funds received, is the best guarantee that can be offered for the disposal of any future ones which may be given to them. The Vicar, The Rev. Thomas Guy, and Churchwardens, grateful for past, with deference and respect, solicit future aid, to enable them to complete the work of restoration.

Howden, January, 1851.

HISTORY OF HOWDEN.

Hereford Cathedral, West Front

HISTORY

OF THE

CHURCH,

PARISH, AND MANOR,

OF

HOWDEN.

Deruentio, qui imbribus auctus & quasi irritatus sæpiùs ripas contemnit, & vicinis pratis superinfunditur, hinc 𝕬𝖗𝖊𝖘𝖍𝖎𝖑𝖑 castrum nitidum, & munitum præteriens quod Thomas Percius Vigorniæ Comes construxerat, velocior sub *Babthorpe* quæ clare Equitum familiæ nomen & mansionem præbet, in Ousam prosilit. Qui iam auctiores vndas trahens delabitur prope 𝕳𝖔𝖜𝖉𝖊𝖓 oppidum mercatorium, cuius celebritas non est ab elegantia, aut frequentia, sed quod nomen territoriolo adiuncto fecerit, (quod 𝕳𝖔𝖜𝖉𝖊𝖓𝖘𝖍𝖎𝖗𝖊 inde dicitur) & Collegiatam iampridem quinque Præbendariorum ecclésiolam ostendat, cui adiunctæ sunt Dunelmensium Episcoporum ædes, qui amplissimas possessiones eò loci habent. E quibus Walterus *Skirlaw* qui floruit circa annum 1390, vt in libro Dunelmensi legitur, *Campanile huius ecclesiæ summæ magnitudinis construxit, vt si fortuita aquarum eueniret inundatio, incolis esset perfugium.* Camden.

HOWDEN:

PUBLISHED BY W. F. PRATT, BRIDGE-GATE,

AND SOLD BY ALL BOOKSELLERS.

MDCCCLI.

First published 1850 and again in 1851.
This facsimile reprint published 1982 from the 1851
edition, by
MR. PYE (BOOKS)
47, Hailgate,
Howden,
Goole. DN14 7ST

ISBN 0 946289 00 X

Printed in Great Britain by
The Moxon Press Ltd,
122 Bolling Road, Ben Rhydding,
Ilkley, West Yorkshire

HOWDEN CHURCH.

THIS holy ground my earliest steps have trod,
When childish musings turn'd my soul to God—
That God who looks o'er all—alas vain man !
Fondly conceiving that thy narrow span
Of life and intellect, may all things know—
Look down and dwell on what thou seest below.—
There childhood rests, and many an aged head,
At last finds quiet with the silent dead :
Here lies the mother—there the daughter's urn—
All wept, all lov'd, when first they sought that bourne,
Whence to return, to mortal ne'er was given,
Earth's ills exchang'd for all the bliss of Heaven.

That broken stone—sad, sad the sculptur'd tale,
Nor love, nor youth, nor beauty could avail
To save the withering flower which lies beneath,
The prey, the prize, of indiscriminate death.

She lov'd and was belov'd—her guileless heart
Beat but for one—and from that one to part
And still live on—nature the strength denied,
She lov'd—she mourn'd—she sicken'd—and she died.
A parent's pride dealt the untimely blow—
Death gave her bliss—to him gave endless woe.

Where now the pride of Prelate and of Priest!
All gone—and only equal with the least
Of those they spurn'd in wantonness of power,
Who weary laden, labour'd through the hour
Of life's short span—then willing sunk to rest,
Borne on the wings of Hope to regions of the blest.

A child, I wander'd mid thy ruin'd walls,
And sad the memories hastening time recalls,
Of all my fleeting visions, hopes, and fears,
When short-liv'd smiles gave place to short-liv'd tears,
As little skill'd to know why sad my soul,
As powerless now that sadness to control:
When tower and turret stood before my view,
The ruin'd choir, the ivy, and the yew,
The crumbling Palace, with its gloomy Hall,
The sculptur'd Gateway tottering to its fall,—
Heraldic scutcheonry, pride's last retreat—
In fragments mouldering at my boyish feet.—

The grave, the legend, which with fear I read,
Telling me wonders of the silent dead
Who slept in quiet 'neath the grassy sod,
To wake, to rise, to meet a judging God.—

Such thoughts were mine—ere love or passion's
    sway,
Clouded the brightness of my opening day,
Ere hope had wither'd to my aching sight,
Ere morn was clouded by the approach of night,
Ere my soul's freshness shrunk from human pain,
Ere friends prov'd false—or beauty sooth'd in vain—
Ere every joy the dearest to my heart,
Lagging came last, the earliest to depart—
Ere love withdrew his sweetly proffer'd bliss,
When all my world was center'd in a kiss,
And the pale cheek was glistening with a tear
Warm from the heart—and still to memory dear—
Ere on the River's brink, when side by side,
Gladly I'd plung'd beneath its sullen tide
A moment rippled by yon Vesper bell,
My wish'd for requiem, and my last farewell—
Ere sad experience taught me with a sigh,
Man and his works are only born to die.

                  ANONYMOUS.

HISTORY OF HOWDEN.

Howden

Is a Market Town of considerable antiquity, and of local importance. It is the capital of the district called Howdenshire, a Wapontake of the East Riding of Yorkshire, and was so antecedently to the conquest. In Doomsday-Book it is written *Hoveden*, and it is there stated that King Edward had the manor, but that now the Bishop of Durham has it.

It is situated on the north side of the Ouse, in a fruitful district, and much of it is in a high state of cultivation. The parish is an extensive one, including several Townships, and a considerable population, but the Wapontake is one of the smallest in the East Riding.

It is probable that its early inhabitants would generally be of Danish extraction, from its close and constant connexion with Denmark. However, Schleswig and Holstein, doubtless furnished us with many

B

names of places, the ordinary terminations of which
are common with these two provinces and the south
part of the East Riding of Yorkshire.

Anterior to the reign of Edward the Confessor,
the Manor and Church of Howden appear to have
been wrested from the Monastery of Peterborough,
in consequence of the non-payment of the tax
called Danegelt, by that monastery. Thus, being
in King's hands after the battle of Hastings, the
conqueror gave the Manor, also the Church with
its members and appurtenances to William Karilepho,
Bishop of Durham.

This prelate shortly afterwards gave the Church
and its appurtenances to the Monastery and Monks
of Durham, the Manor he retained for himself and
his successors. The gift to the Monks was subse-
quently confirmed by a rule of Pope Gregory.

Doomsday-book gives the following description
of the Manor, at the time of the survey :

" Terra Epi. Dunelmensis. In Hoveden fifteen
Caracutes with the berewicks. Hidon (Hive) one
Car. Dunesthorpe (Owesthorpe) one Car. and a
half. Portiton one Car. and three Oxg. Chevede
(Cavil) two Car. and two Oxg. Estricton one Car.
Chelpin three Car. and two Oxg. Bellebi (Belby)
three Car. and two Oxg. Lucusfled (Yokefleet)
half a Car. Cotes (Cotness) half a Car. Saltemersc
six Car. Laxinton one Car. Scilton three Car.
and two Oxg. Bernebelt (Barnhill) one Car. Torp
one Car. and a half. Cledington six Car. Aschilebi
one Car. Barnebi one Car. Babetorp two Oxg."

"There are to be taxed in all, fifty-one Car. six Oxg. and there may be therein thirty ploughs. King Edward had this Manor. The Bishop of Durham now has in the Demesne one plough and sixty-five villanes and twenty-three bordars having sixteen ploughs and three sokemen with two ploughs. In the Manor is a Church and a Priest. Wood pasture three miles long and one broad, The whole Manor six miles long and two broad. Value in King Edward's time forty pounds, at present twelve pounds. All these berewicks are waste."

We have here the old orthography of several of the places within the Manor, and their relative values, as also its extent, and how much of it was reclaimed and cultivated. The reduction of its value from forty pounds in King Edward's time to twelve pounds, at the time of the survey, tells a fearful tale of the ravages which the country had undergone.

The various risings of the Saxon population had so exasperated the Conqueror, that in several districts, it is said, his merciless rage had not left a single human creature, and in Howden Manor, a few years had reduced the value of the Bishop's lands to about one-fourth of their previous rental.

William Rufus having accused William, then Bishop of Durham, of siding with the rebellious Barons, ravaged Howden, Welton, and other places belonging to that see in Yorkshire, and seized the possessions into his own hands. These he granted out to his favourites, Odo, Count of Campania, and

Alan, Count of Richmond. Henry the First afterwards restored them to Ralph the then Bishop.

The Bishop of Durham held all pleas within his liberty of Howdenshire, which he by law might hold in his County Palatine of Durham, pleas of the crown only excepted. The Bishops claimed to have the return of writs and other franchises, as also pleas of law, warrants and other liberties and privileges.

The Manor and its appurtenances appear to have been demised on various occasions, to meet the pressing pecuniary wants of several of the Bishops who held it from time to time.—Bishop Lewis Beaumont made it over to certain foreigners, *alienigeni,* for ten years. Some of the Bishops appear to have appointed Justices of the Peace for Howdenshire.

The Manor has at various times been the subject of forfeiture, of grant, and of re-grant, nevertheless always coming back to the See of Durham. It was in lay hands during the commonwealth, again attached to the See at the restoration. Here it continued till the Bishoprick of Ripon was formed and constituted in 1836, from which time it became an integral part of that See. At what value it was so handed over is only known to those who were parties to similar bargains, which have created no small dissatisfaction and suspicion in the public mind.—It is now nearly eight centuries since it was originally given to the See of Durham.

During the civil wars, Thomas Morton was then

Bishop of Durham, who suffered much, as well in person as in purse.—In May, 1646, after the dissolution of the See, Parliament voted him eight hundred pounds per annum. This he had great difficulty in getting paid, and was ultimately so reduced as to become private tutor in the family of Sir Christopher Yelverton. By this family, especially by the learned Sir Henry Yelverton, who had been his pupil, he was kindly supported till his death.

By an ordinance of the Lords and Commons of the same year, the Manor of Howden, and the possessions of the Bishoprick were vested in trustees for sale, for the benefit of the nation. In July, 1650, these trustees sold the Manor of Howden to William Underwood and Thomas Coghill, for five thousand one hundred and ninety two pounds fifteen shillings.

The Manor includes the two extensive Commons of Bishopsoil and Wallingfen, the former containing two thousand six hundred and twenty-two acres, the latter about five thousand acres.—The Bishopsoil act of Parliament was passed in 1767, and the Wallingfen act in 1777. An annual rent of sixpence per acre was reserved to the Bishop of Durham as lord of the Manor, with the mines and minerals under the whole of the land awarded.

The rights of pasturage over this wide space was claimed by all the parishes and townships abutting thereon, or having right of pasturage upon it, *ratione tenuræ*.

Temp. Hen. 8.   Leland says "Walling Fenne hath many carres of waters in it: and is so bigge that a fifty-eight Villages ly in or abut on it, whereof most part be in Hoveden Lordship, longing to the Bishop of Duresme, and part in Harthil Hundred."

"From Scalby to Hoveden four miles, scant one by enclosed pasture, and three by marishe and fenne ground."

"Certain Chirches do homage of Hoveden Chirch.   There is a Park at Hoveden longing to the Bishop of Duresme, in the way to Bernehill."

"These following be gentilmen of most fame in Hovedenshire, Metham of Metham, Monckton of Cavill, and Portington of Portington."

The Bishop's Palace, he says, "lyeth south of the Chirch, the centre is of tymber, the other three most of stone, and part of bricke." The arms of Skirlaw still remain over the porch, formerly the principal entrance.

The River extent of the Manor is from Cawood to Welton, about thirty miles.   It includes the following parishes and townships, or rather portions of them, in several of which are mesne Manors, some of them dependant on the See, others the fee of private individuals, and not a few of these have fallen into desuetude, by negligence or failure of a sufficiency of tenants legally to uphold them.

Asselby.	Kilpin.
Barmby-on-the-Marsh.	Knedlington.
Belby.	Riccall.
Cliffe-cum-Lund.	Saltmarshe.
Eastrington.	Skelton.
Ellerker-cum-Brantin-	Walkington.
gham.	Welton-cum-Melton.
Howden.	

A considerable portion of the Manor is of the tenure called customary freehold. The fines are small and certain, These customary payments are more vexatious than profitable, and are of inconsiderable amount.

The demese lands of Manor, are considerable, amounting to about thirteen hundred acres. They are almost all in Howden, Saltmarshe, and Skelton. The Rev. J. D. Jefferson, Philip Saltmarshe and William Scholfield, Esquires, are the principal lessees,

A subdivision of the lands in Howden would be of great advantage to the town, and the Bishop of Ripon, if so minded, might not only benefit himself, but confer a great boon on the inhabitants of the place.

Lord Howden, the second bearing that title, is the Steward of the Manor, and he appointed a deputy Steward in January, 1830, neither of whom interferes in the ordinary business of Manor Courts. These duties are performed by Mr. R. B. Porter, of Howden, Solicitor, who is Clerk of the Bishop's

Halmot Court.   He is also Coroner of the Division
of Howdenshire as constituted before the recent
subtraction of some portions of it.   This appoint-
ment is appendant to the Manor.

The palace and grounds around it, ought, on
every account, to be given to the Vicarage, to which
there is no residence.   It may be doubted if the
Prebendal buildings, now being demolished, do not
belong to the Vicar.   By the ordination of March,
1267, it is provided that "the area or *Church-yard*
shall be divided among the Prebendaries, for their
habitation."   When the Church was dissolved, these
buildings and the ground on which they stood, as a
portion of the Church-yard antecedently to the
ordination, would apparently revert to the Vicarage,
when the Prebends became vested in the crown.—
It is clear that they either belong to the grantees of
the Prebends or to the Vicar, as also the ground on
which they stand.

Howdenshire for ecclesiastical purposes was a
Peculiar in the patronage of the Dean and Chapter
of Durham.   This court had jurisdiction over all
causes matrimonial and of divorce, and such as
appertained to health of souls and correction of
morals.   The principal causes of citation were, not
bringing children to be baptized, conventicles in
private houses, adultery, non-repair of the fabrick,
&c.   It pronounced decrees of divorce, a mansâ et
thoro, restitution of conjugal rights, penance, public
and private, &c.   The official was styled " The
Worshipful the Keeper, Vicar General and Official,

Principal of the Spiritual and Peculiar jurisdiction of Howdenshire, &c." William Gray, Esq., M.A. was the last person who filled this dignified situation. The Visitations were always held at Howden.

This Peculiar is now merged in the Archdeaconry of the East Riding. It comprised the following Parishes and Chapelries.

Parishes of Howden.
Eastrington.
Holtby.
Hemingbrough.
Skipwith.
Brantingham.
Welton,
Walkington.

Chapelries of Barmby Marsh.
Barlby.
Blacktoft.
Ellerker.
Laxton.

The 6th and 7th William 4th enacted "That all parishes which are locally situate in one Diocese, and are under the jurisdiction of another, be made subject to the See within which they are locally situate."

This transferred the Peculiar to the Diocese of the Archbishop of York.

The Church,

Which was dedicated to St. Peter, was originally a Parochial Rectory in the patronage of the Prior and Convent of Durham, and so continued till it was made Collegiate in 1267.—The structure, we may safely conclude, stands upon the foundation of a heathen temple, which was probably transformed into a Christian church, during some of those sudden and mysterious conversions of a population which, in whole tribes, were occasionally won over to the true faith, and in a body underwent the rites of baptism.

We know that it had its fair share of shrines, saints, and reliques, in Saxon times. This clearly proves its great antiquity. St. Osara was held in especial favor, and her miracles and shrine had a fame beyond the confines of the kingdom, then known by the name of Anglia. Osara was the sister of Osred, king Northumbria, of which name there were two, in the eighth century. She had a tomb of wood in the church, of which no trace remains. A singular tale is told of her miraculous power, in Gyraldus Cambrensis, to whom we refer the curious reader.

In the Month of March, in 1227, the eleventh year of Henry the Third, Walter, Archbishop of York, with the assent of Fulk Basset, the Parson of

S.W. View of Hawsten Church.

Howden, and the Prior and Convent of Durham,
granted to Walter Kirkham, Clerk, all the tithes
of corn, pertaining to the Chapel of Eastrington,
by name of a single benefice, without cure of souls
or episcopal burthens. An annual payment of three
bezants was reserved to the Parson of Howden,
and his successors, payable on Martinmas-day.

Hugh de Darlington, Prior of the Convent of
Durham, obtained a Bull from Pope Gregory the
Ninth, to appropriate the tithes and emoluments of
the Parish of Howden, for the support of sixteen
Monks. At considerable cost he got this appropri-
ation changed, and converted the Monks into
Prebendaries, thinking the latter would be of greater
use, and more acceptable to the Clergy.

The other parties who joined in the application
for this Bull, and the deed of Ordination which
was founded upon it, were Robert de Stichel, Bishop
of Durham, and Walter Giffard, Archbishop of York.
The following is Hutchinson's translation of this
interesting document.

"March 6th, 1267. Forasmuch as the Parish
of Howden is very wide and large, and the
profits and rents are so much abounding as to be
sufficient for the maintenance of many spiritual
men, therefore, Walter, Archbishop of York, (at
the instance and petition of his Chapter of York,)
that there might be Prebends ordained out of the
revenues of the church, and by their concurrent
authority and consent, and likewise of the submission
of the Prior and Convent of Durham, to him, of

whose patronage it was, made this ordination, viz.
that there should be in this church of Hoveden, five
prebends for ever, and each of them to maintain at
his own proper costs, a priest and clerk in holy
orders, to administer in the same, in a canonical
habit, according to the custom of the church at
York, and to observe the like way of singing, as
those of York church, (except in matins, which
they shall say in the morning for the parish,) and
one of them who is most fit, shall be rector of the
choir, and ordain things belonging to divine service,
and each of them, as an ebdomodary, shall orderly
keep his turn, and serve the cure of the parish by his
respective priest, in the portion assigned to him."

"Moreover, he appointed, that the priests of the
altars of St. Mary, St. Thomas, and St. Catherine
be, in conformable habits present at all canonical
hours, processions, and high masses; and other
altars should in no wise be deputed to the priests
of prebends lest by that means the number of
ministers be diminished, who are rather to be
augmented."

"Likewise he ordained that each of those three
altar priests, should have for their service, in aug-
mentation to their stipends, one mark yearly out of
the obventions of the great altar."

"Also he ordained and granted to the Prior and
Convent of Durham, to be appropriated to their
own use, viz. the chapel of Estrington, with the
profits ecclesiastical of the same town, and of the
towns of Cayvil, Portington, Owsthorpe, Hythe,

Birland, Sandholme and Newland, the land of the Marshal, and the land of the chamber of Limpinhill, Grenhant (or Grenaske) Belassise, and Holy Land (Bennetland) with the tithe of John de Warwick's; together with the sepulture of the parishioners of the said towns and the emoluments and burdens parochial, so as the prebends be for ever free from payment of pensions and procurations."

"And all the residue of the parish of Hoveden should be assigned to the five prebendaries, distinguished as hereafter; and also the obventions of the altar and mortuaries, and personal tithes of those towns deputed to the said prebends, should be converted to the uses of canons, and be amongst them equally divided, which said canons should for three months in the year, at least, make their personal residence in the church, either so long together, or at several times."

"Also the Prior and Convent should have the patronage of the said prebends, and should present the prebendaries to the archbishop, to be by him instituted and inducted, or to the Dean and Chapter of York, in vacancy of the see."

"The area, or churchyard, should be proportionably divided to the prebendaries for their habitations, and the value of the buildings then erected should be converted to the fabric of the quire: and lest any dispute should arise about the order of sitting or presiding, the following manner of sitting in the quire was by the Archbishop ordained."

First, the prebendary of Hoveden, called the first prebendary, shall have the first place.

Second, the prebendary of the third prebend, Thorpe, the second place.

Third, the prebendary of the fifth prebend, Saltmarsh, the third place.

Fourth, the priest of the altar of St. Thomas, the fourth place.

First, the prebendary of the second prebend, Barneby, the first place.

Second, the prebendary of the fourth prebend, Laxton, the second place.

Third, the priest of the altar of St. Mary, the third place.

Fourth, the priest of the altar of St. Catherine, the fourth place.

The same order was to be observed in the processions.

PREBEND OF HOWDEN.

In 1267 the prebend of Howden was ordained the first prebend in this collegiate church, and was freed from all cure of souls, and made a simple and pure prebend only; to be at the presentation of the Prior and Convent of Durham, at every vacation thereof, and to the peculiar maintenance thereof, had assigned all the predial tithes of hay, wool, and lamb, of the towns of Hoveden, Knedlington, and Bernehill.

PREBEND OF BARNEBY.

March 16th, 1267, the prebendary of Barneby was ordained the second prebend, and for the maintenance of the prebendary, was endowed with the tithes of hay, wool, and lamb, of the towns of Barneby and Askelby,

PREBEND OF THORPE.

March 16th, 1267, the prebend of Thorpe was ordained the third prebend in Hoveden church, and was endowed with the predial tithes of hay, wool, and lamb, of the towns of Thorpe, Beleby, Balkholme, Lynton, and Sayre, together with the tithes of that culture *del splen* of Kilpin and Trandikes.

PREBEND OF SKELTON.

In 1267, the fourth prebend in the collegiate church of Howden was that of Laxton and Skelton, which by the ordination, was endowed with the predial tithes of hay, wool, and lamb, of the towns of Laxinton, Skelton, and Gresby. On the 13th of July, 1330, William, Archbishop of York, further ordered, that this Prebend of Skelton, be a simple and pure prebend, and be free from the cure of souls, having a proper Vicar, who should be presentable by the Prior and Convent of Durham.

PREBEND OF SALTMARSH.

In 1267, the fifth prebend in Howden church was that of Saltmarsh, which was endowed with the predial tithes of hay, wool, and lamb, of the towns of Saltmarsh, Coteness, Metham, and Yukeflete. And in April, 1320, William, Archbishop of York, ordained that this prebend should be a simple and pure prebend, free from all cure of souls, and when vacant, be presentable by the Prior and Convent of Durham.

PREBEND OF SKIPWITH.

February 4th, 1279, by the consent of the Prior and Convent of Durham, a sixth prebend called the prebend of Skypwith was ordained, in the collegiate church of Howden, by William Wickwayne, Archbishop of York, to which he assigned all the predial tithes of corn in Skypwith, and the tithe of the hay of the town of Duffield, and appointed this prebend also to have its proper vicar.

The patronage of this prebend was in the Prior and Convent of Durham.

VICARAGE OF HOWDEN.

February 2nd, 1319, William de Melton. archbishop of York, ordained that there be a perpetual vicar in the church of Hoveden, and the vicar thereof should be presented by the Prior and Convent of Durham, and to have cure of souls, which are dependant of the prebend of Hoveden, and should have for his portion the sum of ten pounds sterling, annually paid him out of the profits of the said prebend, by the prebendary for the time being.

VICARAGE OF BARNEBY-UPON-DERWENT,
IN HOWDEN CHURCH.

Barneby, in the parish of Howden, being a prebend within the collegiate church thereof, had, on the 2nd of August, 1322, a perpetual vicarage ordained therein by William de Melton, archbishop of York, who appointed that the vicar thereof should be presented by the Prior and Convent of Durham, and serve in the said prebend, bearing and exercising the whole cure whatsoever, as incumbent on the said prebend: the portion of whose vicarage should consist of ten marks sterling per annum, paid by the prebendary for the time being, out of the fruits of his prebend.

VICARAGE OF THORPE,
IN HOWDEN CHURCH.

The said Archbishop also ordained the vicarage of the prebend of Thorpe, to be a perpetual vicarage in the church of Howden.

VICARAGE OF SKELTON,
IN HOWDEN CHURCH,

On the 13th of July, 1330, the said archbishop ordained a perpetual vicarage in the prebend of Skelton, within the collegiate church of Howden,

D

wherein should be a perpetual vicar presentable by
the Prior and Convent of Durham, the portion of
whose vicarage should consist of ten marks sterling,
per annum, payable by the prebendary of Skelton,
out of the profits of his prebend at Martinmas and
Pentecost by equal portions.

VICARAGE OF SALTMARSH,
IN HOWDEN CHURCH.

In April, 1320, William, archbishop of York,
ordained a perpetual vicarage in the prebend of
Saltmarsh, within the collegiate church of Howden,
and a perpetual vicar thereof, presentable by the
Prior and Convent of Durham, who should have
all cure of souls whatsoever, within the said prebend,
and have allotted for the portion of his vicarage, ten
marks sterling, per annum, out of the profits of the
said prebend, payable by the prebendary for the
time being.

There were several Chantries in Hoveden
Church.

1. St Thomas the Martyr. The Priest whereof
had the fourth Stall on the north side of the Choir,
among the Canons.

2. St. Mary's otherwise Cliff's Chantry. The
Priest whereof had the third Stall on the north
side of the Choir, among the Prebendaries and
Vicars.

3. St. Catherine's Chantry. The Priest of this
Chantry had the fourth Stall on the north side of
the Choir.

4. St. Cuthbert's Chantry.

5. St. Andrew's Chantry. This was founded by Thomas son of Jordan de Metham. This Chantry was endowed with three oxgangs of land, or the rents therefrom, one of them at Askleby, another in Hoveden, and a third in Laxton. The Priest was to perform daily service, and to pray for the souls of the said Thomas and Alice his wife, his parents, and all his ancestors. The arms of Metham point out the position of this Chantry.

There appears to have been a Chapel dedicated to St. Marie Magdalene in Hoveden. There was also a cell or hermitage at Ayngelstone-Hyrst, doubtless Ringstone Hurst. John Richardson, a hermit and of the Franciscan order officiated thereat. He had the grant of a penny a day for life from Bishop Fox, who was consecrated in the year 1494, to be paid to him by the Receiver of the said Bishop for the time being, for his maintenance.

The collegiate church of Howden was dissolved in the first year of the reign of Edward the Sixth, and the temporalities thereby became vested in the crown, in which they remained till the 19th of January, 1582, when queen Elizabeth granted them by letters patent under the great seal of England, to Edward Frost, and John Walker, and others, their heirs and assigns for ever.

Whilst the property remained in the crown it produced a revenue of £40. per annum, but when disposed of to the grantees a rent of £6. 13s. 4d. was reserved, so the crown lost the inheritance of

£33. 6s. 8d. for which ten years purchase was
stipulated to be paid, but was cleared and pardoned
by the statute of 43rd of Queen Elizabeth.

The prebendaries of this church who were
resident, had the glebe, the petty tithes, and Easter
offerings, and were to repair the chancel, to find
bread and wine, and bell ropes, and to keep hospi-
tality.

In the 26th of Henry VIII. the Prebends of
Howden Church, were valued as follows, viz.
Howden £18. 13s. 4d. in the whole, and £12.
clearly. Skelton £15. 13s. 4d. in the whole, and
£9. clearly. Thorpe £16. 11s. 4d. in the whole,
and £9. 18s. 4d. clearly. Saltmarsh £16. 13s. 4d.
in the whole, and £10. clearly. Barmby £16. 6s. 8d.
in the whole, and £9. 13s. 4d. clearly. Skipwith
£18. in the whole, and £13. 6s. 8d. clearly.
There were also six Vicars, besides Chantry priests,
in this Church.

By means of the dissolution of the collegiate
church, the revenues which supported the fabrick in
repair having fallen into private hands, and the choir
becoming totally neglected for a considerable time,
went much to decay, so that in the year 1591, the
parishioners agreed that Mr. Henry Bethell, surveyor
of the Queen, should examine the state of the
chancel, and report the same to the lord treasurer
of England, with a certificate, comprising an account
of the timber, stone, and other articles which would
be necessary to complete the repair of it.

It however appears that nothing of any importance was done in consequence of the above, and the choir continued going gradually to decay, till about the year 1630 it became unsafe to celebrate Divine service in, accordingly the parishioners set about repairing the nave, and in the years 1634 and 1635 great sums were expended in new roofing and stalling that part of the church.

About the middle of the year 1696 the groined stone roof of the chancel fell in, having withstood the ravages of time upwards of three hundred years. Several unsuccessful attempts were made to restore it, but they all proved abortive.

Gent says, "The choir fell down not many years ago. But in the wicked usurper's time, the inner part was miserably rent to pieces; its comely, tuneful, and melodious organ pulled down; some of the vile miscreants, his soldiers, carrying the pipes, and scornfully striving to tune them, as they proceeded towards Wressle, two miles from that place."

On the 7th of October, 1701, the Barons of the court of Exchequer referred the suit of the parish, against those persons who held the revenues of the late dissolved college, for the repairs of the chancel, to the determination of his grace Dr. John Sharp, Archbishop of York, who accordingly made an award under his hand and seal, of which the Rev. Thomas Reynolds, the then Vicar, had a copy from Mr. Dearing his grace's chaplain.

In 1718 the church was greatly ornamented for the reception of Sir William Dawes, Bart. arch-

bishop of York, who at this time held a confirmation
in it.

In 1785 and the following year, the chancel and
chapter-house were cleared of the stones and rubbish
occasioned by the falling of the roof. Just below
the surface of the ground, the workmen found a
stone coffin in which were human bones. The
bones were put into the earth, and the coffin, by the
direction of the vicar and churchwardens, was
placed behind the south door of the cross
aisle.

The church is in the form of a cross, with a
square tower rising from the centre, upon pointed
arches, supported on clustered pillars. There is no
evidence to prove the time of its being built, but it
appears from the great irregularity in placing the
stones, observable in various parts of the walls, that
it hath been erected from the materials of a previous
structure, and it is probable, that as the early
English style of architecture prevailed, when the
Prebends was endowed in 1267, that the Transept
and Nave were then complete, if not more of the
fabrick.

The tower was erected or heightened by bishop
Walter Skirlaw, about the year 1390. This tower
has been stated by various authors, to have been
built for the purpose of the inhabitants to flee to as
a place of safety in case of inundations, which
surmise is ridiculous.

This Bishop also built the Chapter-house and
School, and expended great sums of money in the

Nave

_ as _ proposed _

repairing of Howden church, and on his death in 1405, he left £40. towards the fabrick of the same.

The external portion of the choir has been of much more elegant workmanship than the nave or transept; the east end of the choir is remarkably beautiful, and contains several niches which have been filled with Statues, some of which remain at present.

The pillars forming the aisles are regular, five on each side, supporting pointed arches ; the columns are composed of a cluster of four cylinders, each ribbed in front, the capitals octagonal, the arches of varied character, and the whole, light, well proportioned, and beautiful.

The nave is lighted by three windows to the west, the centre window of four lights ; six windows to the north, and three to the south, three being closed by the porch and school-house, which last is built against that front ; they are all under pointed arches, and composed of three lights each ; with various tracery.

The building of the nave is without much ornament, and with heavy buttresses, the south front being greatly injured by the school-house, which is elevated on a vault of stone, and is ascended by several steps : the windows and door-way of the west end are finished with arches of many kinds, rising from beautiful pilasters, the centre and buttresses terminating in lantern pinnacles, finished with tabernacle work, which gives it a very uncommon appearance. There remain two statues in niches, supposed to be St. Peter and St. Paul,

one supporting a tabernacle, and both of them
in good preservation.

The transept is lighted by a large window at
each end, and two side windows to the west, there
is a door-way which leads into the choir, the
fillets of the arches are ornamented with sculpture.

On each side of the door communicating with
the Choir, are two Statues. They stand on pedestals
in niches, with canopies and tabernacle work. One
of them is St. John the Evangelist, at whose feet is
an eagle with a label in its mouth, on which are the
words *in principio erat.* Another is that of Queen
Emma, mother of Edward the Confessor, with her
eyes bandaged. The other two are the effigies of
St. Peter and St. Paul.

Emma had been successively the wife of the
Saxon King Ethelred and of the Danish King
Canute. On an imputation against her chastity
with Alwine Bishop of Worcester, she is said to
have walked blindfolded over burning ploughshares,
an ordeal not unusual in those days. Her royal
feet showed no blister, and by consequence her
royal character no stain. She died in 1052.

We may possibly owe her presence here to the
fact of Hoveden having been wrested from the
Monastery of Peterborough. Elsine the Abbot
thereof, at the time the severance took place, was
greatly patronized by Emma. Abbot Elsine was a
collector of reliques and objects of taste, in search
of which he resorted to the Continent, and it was
during one of these absences, accompanied by Emma,

or forming one of her train, that the Church was taken from the Monastery, from their neglect to pay the Danegelt, a tax as inglorious and oppressive as ever tyranny exacted from thraldom,

Over the screen is the rood-loft, where the organ was formerly placed. This instrument, it is said, was destroyed by some soldiers of the Parliament in the year 1643, in their way to Wressle Castle. By Gent's account, they paraded about the streets with its pipes, " the vile miscreants," he indignantly says, " Cromwell's soldiers, scornfully striving to tune them as they proceeded towards Wressle."

Near the south-east pillar of the tower is an Altar-tomb, though it is not accurately known to what purposes it was applied. There are nine shields of arms upon it, being probably the arms of such persons as contributed towards the erection or reparation of some portion of the building. Amongst them are those of Buisli, Vesci, Gilbert de Gaunt, Paganel, Wortley, Darcy, Saltmarsh or Dacre, and two others. It is now difficult to recognize them, being partially obliterated, and having no distinctive tinctures. Some persons have conjectured that the Oblations and Easter Offerings were paid on this altar, but I know not on what authority.

From the arms of Gilbert de Gaunt being found here, we may conjecture its date to be as early as Richard the First, for this Gilbert de Gaunt was deprived of his title and estates by

E

King John, in the following reign. We may suppose that those persons whose arms were fixed here
contributed to the building of the transept, if not
to the nave, for this Altar and the part of the
Church in which it stands, are in all likelihood of
co-eval workmanship.

The Lantern Tower is a noble structure, and the
effect is remarkably good, being lighted by tall and
handsome windows, of the purest perpendicular
character. A question has been mooted how much
of this Tower was built by Skirlaw. It would
appear that he raised it from the base as high as
the top of the large windows, a work probably
completed in his life time, for his arms are found
between the upper part of the windows to the east,
on a level with the springing of the arch and below
the point of it. The sum left by his will, we may
suppose expended on the highest section of the
Tower. These windows are louvered and the
arches of them depressed, and out of character
with the general architecture of the fabrick, being
of the same style as those of the School, towards
both of which he contributed by his will. Had
they been completed during his life time, we may
safely conclude his nice taste would have suggested
something more effective, and consonant in taste
and propriety with such works as we know to have
been erected under his own eye. This upper section
of the Tower is the belfrey, and has apparently been
erected sometime after the Lantern Tower, to which
it is rather an excresence than an improvement.

Within the Lantern Tower are the arms of Skirlaw to the east, as stated above. To the south are those of Metham; to the west the arms of Bishop Langley; and to the north, apparently, those of Bishop Kirkham. There is also on the same level with these, a shield of arms in each corner. To the north east, on a fess, three buckles: to the south east, three roses, probably Darcy: to the south west, on a band, three escallops: and to the north west, on a bend, three buckles. These are all well executed and in excellent preservation, and are some of them doubtless the arms of persons who aided Skirlaw in the work. Others were probably placed there, as having been antecedently Prelates friendly to, or more immediately benefactors of the Church and Town of Howden.

On the north side of the transept towards the south, are the remains of two chantreys, now thrown into one. They were the burial place of the Metham family, their arms are found in the wall, as also those of Hamilton with whom they intermarried. The recumbent figures found here, were originally in the choir. Two of them are Methams, the other is a Saltmarsh. The piscinas remain, and the division walls may yet be traced. The whole is now, and has long been used as the burial place of the family of Philip Saltmarsh, Esq.

The corresponding chantries to the north, are now hardly traceable. The connecting arches are bricked up, and the chantries themselves are roof-

less. The Saltmarsh chantry now covered with
slate, and having a roof so much out of character
with the edifice, is an eyesore to its external appearance.

The choir, though now in ruins, had side aisles
similar to the nave, and when perfect must have
been extremely beautiful. There are six windows
on each side, of varied tracery. The large
east window was remarkably fine, and the effect of
it, and the two smaller side windows, as seen from
the west end of the Church, must have been strik-
ing in the extreme.

The choir fell down in 1696, having long been
disused for the purposes of devotion, from a fear of
its insecurity and danger.

It begets a melancholy feeling, to stand amidst
this ruin, mouldering piecemeal to decay, and now
the burial place of many of those whose progenitors
witnessed its fall, possibly without one pang of
regret.

It is greatly to be regretted that no trace or
vestige of the shrine of St. Osara remains to mark
its position. We know who she was, and that her
fame was greatly extended. The virgin sister of a
king, canonized by a superstitious Church for the
adoration of a still more superstitious people, is
supposed to have had worshippers of a class similar
to those of the following legend. Virgin purity
and youthful loveliness, seeking in fulness of heart,
to create and share a happiness which, when found
we are told, is always born a twin.

The Song of St. Osara.

ALL hail to Saint Osara!
  To thee our praise be given!
Once fairest of Northumbria's maids,
  And now a saint in Heaven!
With flowers we deck thy holy Shrine,
  With rose, and may, and yarrow,
Here, on thy virgin votaries smile,
  Sweet, gentle Saint, Osara!

Look on the land where once thou dwelt,
  Thy worshippers implore thee—
At the same Shrine our mothers knelt,
  Our daughters shall adore thee.
Our hearts we offer at thy Shrine,
  Then find those hearts a Marrow
As true and loving as our own,
  Kind, gentle Saint, Osara.

On Saint Mark's witching eve we'll search
  The holy church-yard thorough,
And garland round our youthful heads,
  With flowers of blooming yarrow—
We'll sing the song our mothers sung,
  "Sweet yarrow now I find thee,
Thy witching power I know, I feel—
  My lover stands behind me."

"Sow, sow the hemp—cast, cast it round,
    Speed, speed the spell I'm waking—
The solemn bell of midnight tolls—
    Cease, cease my heart from aching.
Now hemp, now yarrow, work your charm,
    Aid, aid my bold endeavour,
Give me his heart, I've lost my own,
    And make him mine for ever."

"I hear his step, I feel his breath,
    He's mine in joy and sorrow,
I may not see his face to-night,
    He'll smile on me to-morrow."
Oh then sweet Saint, we'll bless thy name,
    Me and my faithful Marrow,
Fresh flowers we'll bring and incense burn,
    To our kind Saint, Osara!

Doubtless the fabrick was at one time an object of pride with the parishioners at large. The Reformation, dissent, and diversity of religious faith have done their work. We have heard a very old lady, now no more, say, it was the custom annually before the October fair, to wash and brush up the tower by men suspended in baskets from the top, a practice long discontinued.

About the year 1840 and since that time, great improvements and reparations have been made in various parts of the fabrick. The ruined part was secured by clamping it with iron, by filling up the interstices, and by putting in new stones for those

Chancel

looking East

decayed, and by rendering it as secure as its delapi-
dated state would admit of. It may thus remain
secure for many years, with ordinary attention, but
the east end must be always considered at the
mercy of the elements.

At this period two side screens were thrown
across the transept. Steps were raised of figured
encaustic tiles in front of the Altar, and the Deca-
logue was newly and beautifully lettered and
inserted in the recess of the door-way to the Choir.

The space above the screen was filled up with
stained glass by Wailes, having the effigies of the
Virgin, St. Peter, and St. Cuthbert. The stone
screen was also partially repaired.

The floors were removed from the lantern tower,
and the lower windows were glazed, having been
previously filled up with plaster. This is a very
great improvement, and the effect of the Tower as
seen internally is very good. We would however
see the unseemly and misplaced painting of the
Lord's Supper taken from its elevated and unmean-
ing situation.

The organ was removed and two unsightly lofts
were taken down. Till the present gallery on the
north side of the nave be removed, we cannot allow
that the work of restoration is complete. It cannot
be viewed with patience, and its removal should be
the next, and an early step, in the progressive
improvements which have been made and which
yet remain to be done.

Stained glass was put into the three south

windows of the nave in 1841, as also into other
windows of the building.   Of the three named,
beginning with the one eastward, the first contains
the arms of Saltmarsh, Sotheron, Bethell, Empson,.
Worsop, and Estcourt.   The middle window contains
the Royal Arms, those of the Archbishop of York, the
Bishop of Ripon, Lord Hotham, Viscount Galway,
and Lord Howden.   The third window, those of
Clarke, Dunn, Jefferson, Thompson (Lord Wenlock,)
Athorpe, Wyndham, Menzies, and Broadley.

The Chapter House is on the south side of the
Choir.   It is small, being twenty-four feet across,
but very beautifully proportioned.   There are seven
windows of three lights each, with pointed arches
and varied tracery.   There are thirty-four seats
round the interior, the form is octagonal, and the
whole is rich in the extreme, in tabernacle work,
canopies, niches, and every specious of ornament
into which stone can be cut.   Fully to appreciate
its beauty, it must be seen, words cannot convey an
adequate picture of it.   Its groined roof and spire
fell down on St. Stephen's day, 1750.

Hutchinson regarded this Chapter House as the
finest specimen of pointed architecture in England.
" Whilst," he says, " it is the greatest disgrace to
suffer this building to go to decay, we acknowledge
that we have seen nothing in this island of such
elegant work in stone, except at Melrose Abbey, in
Scotland, with which this small building may
justly vie, and in one particular it excels any part in
the Scottish Abbey, by its exquisite and exact

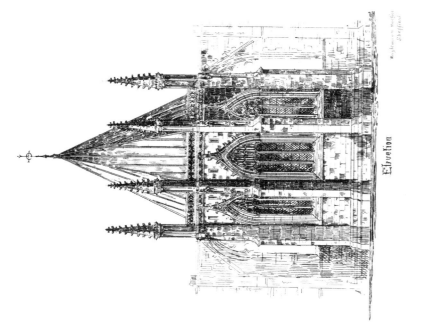

Chapter House
as restored

Section

Elevation

proportions, being the most perfect example of pointed architecture we ever saw."

This is certainly very high praise, yet we do not think it overdone, and it may be looked upon as the chef-d'œuvre of Bishop Skirlaw, that man of exquisite taste and equal magnificence. We may add, and not widely deviate from the truth,

**Ut rosa flos florum,
Sic domus ista domorum.**

A recent writer appears to be of this opinion. We give his words from a small pamphlet published in 1843, and addressed to the Bishop of Ripon.

"I speak in no exagerated terms when I assert —indeed, I only reiterate the opinions of others— that the Chapter House, for elegance and beauty of proportion, stands without an equal among the ecclesiastical structures of Great Britain. Roslyn may be more elaborate and highly finished in its details, York may be larger, and some others may excel it in one or two particulars, but taken as a whole there is nothing equal to it, or capable of being put into competition with it. In finish and proportion it is perfect. It is universally admitted that no where can the architect find specimens of tracery, of mullion, of ornament, better worthy of his study, more perfect in all their parts, or more complete as a whole. It is faultless, and cannot be viewed, even by the eye of indifference, without delight. Such is the opinion of Grose, of Pennant, of Allen, of Britton, and many others. It is, in

F

fine, the chef-d'œuvre of Bishop Skirlaw, that
munificent patron of architecture, ere the art had
been debased by speculations without rules, and by
those mongrel performances too commonly the
coinage of modern brains. We are traditionally
told that this Chapter House was the especial
favourite of the good Bishop, of whose unceasing
kindness to the town of Howden we have a prover-
bial expression among us which survives to this
day, evincing, my Lord, the strength and durability
of our gratitude for such favours as we may receive.
Skirlaw died about the year 1400, and with him fell
much, if not all, of that pure architectural taste
which through four successive centuries of general
and national improvement, has found no revival.
If we may judge by the modern architectural specimens yearly rising up in England and Scotland, the
dawn of a better day is even yet far distant. Is it
not, then, well, my Lord, to preserve this admittedly
perfect building from mouldering into dust and
nothingness? Should not some exertion be made
to save for the study, as well as for the admiration,
of those from whom we may hope for a revival of
the pure spirit of Skirlaw architecture, this beautiful
object? The recent disaster at York is a heavy
blow and great discouragement to us, who are so
unfortunate in the means of making our views and
wishes known to the public. We have received
assurances from individuals, and some societies of
taste and antiquarianism, that our object requires
only to be known to find support. It is through

your Lordship's respected name I now make that appeal, and that I make known the steps already taken towards the restoration of these ruins, and I feel satisfied that this appeal, moderate, very moderate in its extent, will not be made in vain."

The various restorations and alterations were carried out under the skilful direction of Messrs. Wightman and Hadfield, Architects, of Sheffield, and they deserve great commendation. The expences were met by a voluntary subscription, wherein the parishioners were liberally supported by individuals of taste in every part of England, by the Yorkshire Architectural Society, and by other similar Societies. The Rev. Thomas Guy, M.A. the Vicar of Howden, employed his wonted energy therein, and he was very warmly supported by the unwearied exertions of his Church-warden, Mr. John Sugden. The latter, who has been Church-warden many years, has bestowed upon the Fabrick a persevering and unwearied attention, only met with in those whose heart is in the object they undertake, and whose enthusiasm overcomes every difficulty and deficiency.

If a somewhat onerous rate have occasionally caused a heavy grumble, the parishioners may console themselves with the assurance that they have a Church of rarely equalled beauty.—Nay more, such an object daily before their eyes, cannot fail to nourish their taste, to humanize their minds, and to reward them a hundred fold for any call that has been made upon their purses.

On the left, on entering the Chapter House, is a small Chantry, conjectured to be that of St. Thomas. The piscina remains, and over the north window are the arms of Skirlaw and others. This Chantry is now by faculty, the property and burial place of the family of Thomas Clarke, Esq. of Knedlington.

The south porch of the nave has been converted into a Vestry. It is inconvenient, ill-placed, and out of character, for such a purpose. Nevertheless it is an improvement upon the late one, which was in the Choir, and entered under the screen from the transept, a most unseemly excrescence, and very properly removed when the ruins were repaired.

Over the present Vestry, which has an elegant groined roof, is the Muniment Room of the Manor, containing the Court Rolls and other manorial documents. In the centre of the arch, the entrance into this Vestry externally, is the Head of Henry the third, in whose reign it is probable the nave was constructed.

The tower is a beautiful and well proportioned structure. Some part of it, we know, was constructed by Bishop Skirlaw. It includes eight shields of arms, probably of those persons who aided the good Bishop in its erection.

The arms of Skirlaw are to the east, those of Metham to the south, those of Langley to the west, and those of Kirkham, apparently, to the north. There is also a shield of arms in each corner. On one of these are three roses, another has, on a bend three escallops, a third, on a bend three buckles, and the fourth, on a fess three buckles. An ascent to the lantern tower will well repay the exertion. It is very beautiful, in excellent preservation, the shields of arms are perfect, and the tall windows of the purest perpendicular character.

What portion of the tower was really constructed during the life-time of the Bishop, has been the subject of conjecture. As his arms are found between the springing of the arches of the lower windows, it seems probable that he raised the Tower from its base to the upper portion of the large windows. Perhaps we may conclude the bequest in his will was applied to the construction of the upper part, now the belfrey. This is made more probable from its being of the same character as the school, both of them having the depressed arch, and not at all in unison with the perpendicular style of the fabrick. In fact we cannot conceive that a person of such exquisite taste, as we know him to have been, would have tolerated either one or the other.

Skirlaw died in 1403, and left by his will forty pounds *" in fabricatione Campanilis Ecclesiæ de Hoveden."* It is often said that the tower was raised so high as to prove a refuge for the inhabitants in case of floods. Doubtless a joke of some witling from a higher locality. Yet Skirlaw is not unremembered by the inhabitants of Howden, and the following distich on him may occasionally be heard,

" Bishop Skirlaw was good to the people,
  He built them a School-house, and rais'd them
     their Steeple."

The Church has a fine Organ, purchased, and
improved at various times, by voluntary subscription, at a cost from first to last, of nearly one
thousand pounds.

The Church contains few monuments of any note.
Some to the families of Dunn, of Scholfield, of
Jefferson, Worsop, and others, but none of any great
antiquity. There are two slabs in the floor of the
transept, bearing date the year 1673. One to
Nathaniel and another to Stephen Arlush, of
Knedlington. The latter was " *in hâc Ecclesiâ
Concionator optimus,*" the former " *legis procurator
integerrimus, justus et æqui tenacissimus.*" The
name and race are extinct in this neighbourhood.

There is also a fulsome monument in the same
part of the Church to the memory of Captain
Jefferson. The history of this inscription will
be found in Bentley's Miscellany, for March, 1849.
The truthfulness of the inscription may fairly be
considered on a par with the taste of the design.
It is said to have cost considerably upwards of one
thousand pounds.

There is a peal of eight bells, of a particularly
sweet and musical tone. They were cast by Messrs.
Pack and Chapman, of London, and were opened on
Friday, the 14th day of July, 1775. This peal is
well worthy of its reputation, though bell-ringing

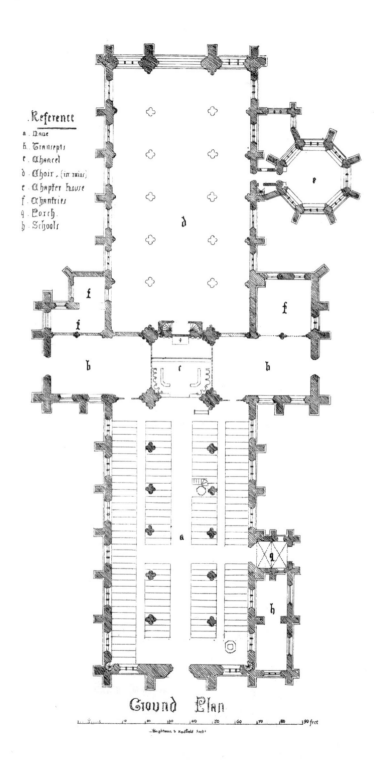

Reference

a. Nave
b. Transepts
c. Chancel
d. Choir, (in ruins)
e. Chapter house
f. Chantries
g. Porch
h. Schools

Ground Plan

Weightman, & Hadfield Arch.ts

has somewhat ceased to be the popular amusement it once was.

The Church is repaired by annual assessments, raised and levied on the several townships. This rate is of so early a date as now to be unequal and unfair, and it certainly requires adjustment. Its arranged proportions were made shortly after the Reformation.

The dimensions of the Structure are,

Length of Nave. . . . . . . 112 feet.
Breadth of ditto. . . . . . . 60 „
Length of Transept.. . . . . 117 „
Breadth of ditto. . . . . . . 30 „
Length of Choir. . . . . . . 112 „
Breadth of ditto. . . . . . . 60 „
Height of Tower. . . . . . 135 „

A font of florid gothic character was recently presented to the Church, by Mr. Henry Rogerson, of Bramley. The gift, a tribute of admiration to the fabrick, was presented through Thomas Clough, Esq. one of the Churchwardens.

The following is a list of the Vicars of Howden :

1320. Dr. Thomas Thorogolt, presented by the Prior and Convent of Durham.

John de Oustrope.

1322. John de Gripthorpe, vacated p. m.

1341. John de Galmeton.

John Skarlett, m.

1362, John de Esyngton, m.

1370. William de Rilleston, pbr.
1404. Rob. de Pokelington, pbr. res. pro. Eccld.
      de Brodsworth.
      William de Aughton, pbr. res. pro. vic. de
      Galmeton.
      John Porter, pbr. res. pro. vic. de Wyston.
1411. Thomas Lister.
      William de Riccal, pbr.
1449. John Hubbersty, res.
1466. Ds. William Waryn, cap. m.
1479. William Belle, cap. res.
1484. Richard Cooke, cap. m.
1485. John Hesington, A.M. res.
1491. Robert Robinson, pbr. m.
1507. Robert Clark, pbr. res.
1517. Robert Cole, pbr. res.
1527. John Wawen, pbr. res.
1535. Miles Whitefeld.
1679. Thomas Reynolds, pr. by the King, res.
1707. Richard Cotton or Coulton, A.B. pr. by the
      King.
1726. Thomas Thirkeld.
1746. James Godmond, m.
1798. Ralph Spofforth, A.M. m.
1825. Thomas Guy, A.M.

The Register of the Parish commences with the
year 1541. The early portion of it is kept in five
divisions, corresponding with the five prebends, as
the Vicar of each Prebendary had cure of Souls
in his own district. It is in good preservation·

A list of collections with the several amounts are given. They were principally made for the re-building of churches having suffered from fire or otherwise, in various parts of the kingdom. Some, are for ransoming captives from slavery under the Turks, for which the sum of £5 3s. 5d. was raised in 1680· We rescue captives by different means in our days, and we may hence conclude that the nation is more powerful, if not more prosperous and happy. A liberal collection was made in 1666, for the great fire in London.

During the Commonwealth marriages were performed by the Justices at their ordinary meetings in Howden, or at the private residences of the Justices. The Justices of that day, generally acting for Howdenshire, were Captain Charles Fenwick, of Hagthorpe, who had been in the service of the Parlia-ment, and Mr. Philip Saltmarshe, of Saltmarshe.

At the time of the Dissolution, this Church was rich in the following Reliques amongst others. A piece of wood from the Cross of the Lord. A piece from the Cross of St. Andrew. Some dust of the bones *"pulvis ossium"* of St. John the Baptist. The hand of St. John the Evangelist. A certain bone of St. Lawrence, another of St. Thodore. Some of the hair of the Virgin Mary, and a piece of the Cradle of the Lord, " *cunabula domini*." Some of the vestments of St. Thomas the Martyr, of St. Leonard, of St. Cuthbert. A bone of St. Sebastian, and of St. Clement. What became of these various riches it would now be vain to conjecture.

G

The Parish consists of the following Townships, with the population of each, in 1841.

Howden......................... 2332
Asselby. 293
Barmby-on-the-Marsh Chapelry.... 506
Balkholme.................... 165
Belby........................ 58
Cotness...................... 38
Kilpin 393
Knedlington................. 142
Laxton Chapelry.............. 266
Metham...................... 42
Saltmarshe.................. 157
Skelton..................... 212
Thorpe...................... 50
Yokefleet 206

A Committee of Justices for the East Riding of Yorkshire, under the provisions of 8 and 9 Victoria, cap. 111, in November, 1847, ordered that every parish and township in the Division of Howdenshire, should hereafter be assessed to the County Rate for the said East Riding, in the following proportions.

	£.	s.	d.
Asselby	8	9	0
Balkholme	5	12	11
Barmby Marsh	14	4	2
Belby	3	14	0
Blacktoft	13	11	9
Bellasize	10	13	9

	£.	s.	d.
Cotness	4	0	5
Eastrington	16	1	6
Gilberdike	11	10	4
Howden	43	14	6
Kilpin	7	8	4
Knedlington	5	17	0
Laxton	7	14	1
Metham	5	15	6
Newport	3	16	1
Portington and Cavill	8	14	5
Saltmarshe	7	6	6
Skelton	11	2	6
Scalby	7	18	7
Thorpe	1	18	1
Wressle, Loftsome, Newsholme, and Brind	23	14	11
Yokefleet	6	13	3
£	229	11	7

This assessment was made on the full letting
value of the property of the East Riding, including
a mileage value on the Railroads and Stations in
every Township. The assessment so made was then
reduced to one penny in the pound, which reduction
gave for the Division of Howdenshire the above
result. Great irregularity had heretofore existed,
but the rate now fixed upon is as just and equitable
as can be arrived at.

The Palace,

Now converted into a farm house, was the favourite residence of many of the Bishops of Durham. Pudsey died here in March, 1194, and his remains were taken to Durham for interment. Kirkham died in this Palace, in August, 1260. He was embowelled here, and his remains were also carried to Durham.

A stone slab in the transept, near the north west pillar of the tower, covered so much of the latter Prelate as remained at Howden, The inscription round its edges has given rise to some acrimony and more dispute. Upon it is a cross flory, and the inscription, though greatly obliterated, clearly bears the name of Kirkham. He had previously been Dean of York.

Walter Skirlaw died at Howden, 1405. He also was embowelled here, and afterwards taken to Durham for interment. This celebrated Bishop and good man, was translated from Bath and Wells to Durham, in 1388. Skirlaugh in the Parish of Swine, in the East Riding of Yorkshire, was his birth place, and there he built the Chapel which still remains, a monument worthy of a man as illustrious for his munificence, as he was famous for his skill and taste in architecture.

He raised the tower of Howden Church, he

Gateway. Bishops. Palace. Howden.

Howden: Published by W. F. Pratt. 1834.

spent large sums of money on the Fabrick, and he constructed that architectural gem, the Chapter House. He also built the large Hall in the Palace, which he made his frequent residence. He was ultimately buried at Durham, where a sumptuous monument was placed over him, worthy of his liberality and his fame.

Thomas Langley, the successor of Skirlaw, had held the great seal, which he resigned when he became Bishop of Durham, in 1406. In 1411 he obtained a Cardinal's Hat from Pope John the twenty-third. He also made great improvements in the Manor of Howden. We are told that " he built the western gates to the Cemetery yard, with a beautiful lodge adjoining, where his arms were placed." This gateway and the arms still remain.

The celebrated Cuthbert Tunstall was Bishop of Durham at the Reformation. He succeeded Wolsey who died at Leicester on his way to London. Tunstall was translated from London in 1530, and he continued to hold his elevated situation through many disastrous years, and many and various persecutions, in the successive reigns of Henry the Eighth, Mary, Edward the Sixth, and Elizabeth. In 1559, he was deprived of his See, and he was placed in the custody of Parker, Archbishop of Canterbury.

This Bishop was probably the last who made Howden his residence, and an agreeable retreat he must have found it, from such great mental and political disquiet as we know he underwent. He was an author of some repute, an astute Ambassador,

and Maître Rabelais has handed him down to
European fame, for his great skill "*in arte suppu-
tandi*," the title of a book written by the Bishop.

He was greatly, at one period of his life, opposed
to the Reformation, and when Ambassador in
Holland, he bought up all the copies of the Scrip-
tures then recently translated into English, and had
them committed to the flames. This was said to have
been a trap laid for the astute Priest, for by it the
translator raised money to pay his debts, and he put
himself in a situation to send forth fresh copies.

He bore three combs upon his shield, and was
said to have been descended, subject to a band
sinister, from the Barber of William the Conqueror.

Near the Palace were the Prebendal Residences,
now being demolished. They had stood nearly four
centuries, and from the difficulty experienced in
tearing them to pieces, they might probably have
stood four more. They resembled some of our older
colleges, and presented a pleasing and characteristic
sight, leading the contemplative mind agreeably
back to the manners and days of a far distant date.

The Bishop of Ripon and his lessee the Rev.
J. D. Jefferson, are removing these very interesting
remains to a distance from the town, and converting
the materials into barns and stables. No one can
witness this needless act of destruction without pain.
It is now too late to call upon any of the numerous
Architectural Societies, established through the
length and breadth of England for the special
preservation of such structures, to ward the blow,

This most interesting monument of the olden time
has ceased to exist. The Lord of the Manor
has pronounced its doom, and the spirit of
that good Bishop who did so much for posterity,
may possibly look down in sorrow now, on what he
once eyed with pleasure and delight.

How wide the difference between the Howden of
that day and the present. In the fifteenth century the
quiet Market Town had residing within its narrow
bounds a Bishop of Durham, almost equally potent in
spiritual and temporal power. Around him might
be assembled the six Prebendaries of the Church,
each of whom supported a Vicar for the performance
of those parochial and spiritual duties which come
within our notion of having the *cure of souls*.
Again, there were the five Chantry Priests, with a
herd of inferior dependents, as Chaplains, Clerks,
Choristers, Vergers, and so on, to the lowest grade
of this imposing Hierarchy.

No wonder the spiritual welfare of the parish
was fully cared for, and their mental and conscien-
tious backslidings, when under the care of these holy
men, would rarely escape detection. Yet it may be
doubted if even all these safeguards were efficacious
for all the purposes of human weakness and human
infirmity. At least we are not given to understand
that such was the case.

The Reformation saw all these swept away, and
with them their wealth, their possessions, and their
dignified and imposing ceremonies—all fell. It is
hardly conceivable what the immediate effect must

have been, till necessity had quietly and silently made other provision for the wants and weaknesses of a people as ignorant as superstitious; and who had hitherto blindly and implicitly left their consciences and their eternal interests in the keeping of the Roman Catholic Priesthood. They were now for the first time to walk by themselves, and we may feel sure that their steps would betray all the tottering and uncertain weakness of infancy. And so it proved, till that which had been so suddenly swept away was supplied from other sources and by other means.

What now has the Church of Howden in the place of this grand array of dignity and wealth? It has one Vicar or Perpetual Curate, subsisting upon a stipend utterly insufficient for the maintenance and support of himself and family, in a state becoming a Christian Pastor.

This Pastor has no residence, no house, and so complete has been the subversion and the change, that he has been almost compelled to leave the Town of Howden, and to take up his abode in the Village of Barmby, where he has lived during the last few years. It was hoped that some arrangement would have been made a short time ago, to annex the Palace and the adjoining Grounds to the Vicarage of Howden, and the Ecclesiastical Commissioners are said to have been in treaty for the purchase of this property for that desirable object. This treaty unfortunately fell to the ground, and very much it is to be regretted, for such an opportunity may never again occur.

Howden.

This Township including Howden-dyke, contains
two thousand three hundred and thirty two inhabitants, and two thousand eight hundred acres of
land, for the most part of good quality, and in
fair cultivation, but capable of great improvement.
The town is of considerable antiquity, it is well built,
paved, flagged, and lighted with gas. Indeed its
neatness, cleanliness, and general appearance are
highly creditable to the inhabitants, and it forms a
pleasing contrast to the Howden of forty years ago.

This improvement is not confined to appearances
only, for the district is certainly more healthy than
formerly, and yet much remains to be done on the
score of sanitary measures. It was visited by
cholera in 1849, but the ravages of the disease were
principally confined to the Union Workhouse.

It has no particular trade or manufacture, and
the inhabitants are dependent on the surrounding
neighbourhood which makes it its ordinary market,
but which has been considerably damaged by the
opening of the Hull and Selby Railway.

Another source of profit to the town, is the
annual horse-fair, perhaps the largest in England.
So early as the year 1200, King John granted a
licence to Philip de Poictou, Bishop of Durham, to
hold an annual fair at Howden, on the second and

H

following day of October. The fair is held in a
field near the town, but the general business extends
over a full fortnight, and is carried on in every town
and village around, as well as in the town of
Howden. Many thousand pounds are annually left
in the neighbourhood, and the innkeepers and
tradesmen consider it their harvest.

The fair appears to have been attended by
foreigners from a very early date, and even now
every kingdom in Europe occasionally sends agents
to it, and its reputation is probably as great as ever.
The number of horses bred in the immediate neighbourhood is not so great as formerly. The number
might in these times be increased, doubtless with
advantage to the farmer, especially if more skilful
attention were given to the selection of suitable
brood mares. This fair attracts a great number of
visiters of all grades and characters, exhibiting every
variety of flat and sharp, the buyer and the seller,
the dealer and his cad, the cheater and the cheatee,
most dishonest effrontery and the most marvellous
simplicity.

There is a spacious Wesleyan Chapel. There
are Independent, Baptist, Primitive Methodist,
Sandemanian Chapels, and other places of public
worship. In September, 1850, the foundation stone
of a Catholic Chapel was laid in a field on the road
leading to Knedlington. The procession threaded
the streets of Howden in a long array of professors
of that religion, where mitre and cross, taper and
stole, attracted the wondering gaze of the spectators.

This might well be so, for full three hundred years had passed since the like was seen, and many looked on with painful rather than with pleasurable emotions.

There is an excellent Lock-up, the residence of the Inspector of Police for the division of Howden-shire. A public building is being erected in the Church-yard, which is intended for a Savings' Bank, a Mechanics' Institute, and also for the Magistrates of the district. This convenience has long been wanted, and the structure will be at once ornamental and useful. The foundation stone was laid on the 12th of August, 1850. The sum of nearly twenty thousand pounds is deposited in this bank, by a great variety of the poorer classes of society. Thomas Clarke, Esq. is the President, William Scholfield and William Dyson Esqrs. are the Vice-Presidents.

There are also various Benefit and Friendly societies, some of them of a very early date. A spring fair was established some years ago, and will probably be found to answer. At this fair the Howdenshire Agricultural Society holds its meetings, when premiums to a considerable amount are annually awarded. The show of horses is generally very good, and the amount of business done at the fair is annually on the increase. With suitable encouragement from the surrounding farmers its success may be considered certain. Mr. William Carter has long been its efficient and able secretary. He liberally allows the contending parties to exhibit

their horses and stock in a field near his own house.
Mr. James Campbell is the honorary treasurer.

Some years since a Court of Sewers was held
here, having existed from the time of Henry the
Eighth, with some slight intervals. It was desig-
nated "the Court of Sewers for Howdenshire, and
for the west parts of the East Riding of the County
of York." Its jurisdiction was a very extensive one,
and unfortunately the last commission was allowed
to expire, *effluxo tempore*, and it has not been
renewed. The agriculturists should use every effort
for its restoration, unless they can secure, what
would be of much greater utility, a drainage act for
the district. This great desideratum has been
attempted several times, and has as frequently failed,
either from the inertness, the ignorance, or the
peevish obstruction of those who ought to be the
foremost in its support.

Howden gives the name to the poor-law union
of Howdenshire. It is very extensive, embracing
forty townships, and forty-one elected Guardians,
there being two for Howden. It includes the
parishes of Howden, Holme-on-Spalding-Moor,
Bubwith, Aughton, North Cave, Blacktoft, Eastrington, Ellerton, and portions of Hemingbrough and
other parishes, with a population of 14,200.

The Union was formed in February, 1837, by the
assistant poor law commissioner, William Revens,
Esq. Thomas Clarke, Esq. was chosen Chairman, the
Rev. Thomas Guy, M.A. Vice-Chairman, and Mr.
George England, Solicitor, the Clerk of the Board

of Guardians. The last named gentleman continues his efficient services, and the neighbourhood owes him and the elected Guardians a debt of gratitude, to which they are fully and honourably entitled. Enabled to speak from personal administration of the old and the new poor-law, the writer hesitates not to declare that the poor are not only much more considerately cared for, that their comforts have increased, and what is best of all, that there is an increased and improved spirit of independence and self reliance, and by consequence greater efficiency and extended happiness and content. A spacious Union Workhouse was erected in 1839. It presents none of the prison like appearance which won for these structures the unfortunate sobriquet of Bastilles. The one in question is a pleasing, cheerful, and ornamental structure, built by Messrs. Weightman and Hadfield, Architects, Sheffield.

Roger de Hoveden is supposed to have been born here, in the time of Henry the Second. His history commences in the year 731, where Bede's ends, and concludes with the third year of John, 1201. It is of great authority, and was much relied upon by Edward the First, in his endeavour to establish his claim historically to the Scottish crown, homage and fealty being claimed therefrom by this arrogant and encroaching Monarch. It is not yet too late for the inhabitants to mark their estimation of their renowned townsman by erecting some monument appropriately dedicated to his memory.

Asselby, Aislabie or Aschilebi,

Is a Constabulary of considerable extent, containing 293 inhabitants. It is of great fertility, and contains many fruit gardens, the produce of which is sent to the West Riding of Yorkshire. It is almost exclusively the property of Thomas Clarke, Esq. as is also the manor or reputed manor, the tithe rent charges, mortuaries, and other ecclesiastical charges, as enjoyed by the Prebendary of Barmby, of which Asselby formed a part. Here was a manor at the time of the Conquest, and Nigel had lands here and five Fisheries, paying annually two thousand eels.

Asselby was the birth place of the Rev. J. Noble, who was born in 1611, and educated at Christ's College, Cambridge. He held St. Giles' Church at Pomfret, till driven out by the act of uniformity. Calamy says that he was a great appeaser of the tumults of his times, that he was an excellent character, a profound divine, and a good man.

The Rev. Thomas Powell, Wesleyan Minister, was also born in this Village. By great assiduity and pains he from great poverty and privation became a learned man. His "Essay on Apostolical Succession," is a work of learning and erudition. He died at Beverley in 1850, the victim of an o'erlaboured mind.

Barmby-on-the-Marsh,

A Chapelry and Constabulary. It contains 506 inhabitants, is an extensive township of upwards of 1700 acres of fertile land, and is almost surrounded

by the rivers Ouse and Derwent. It gave name to
a Prebend in the Church, which was granted by
Queen Elizabeth to the family of White of Walling-
wells. Thomas Clarke, Esq. is the principal
proprietor of the land, as also the owner of the
manor, mortuaries, offerings, and tithes, as enjoyed
by the Prebendary of the Collegiate Church. Earl
Fitzwilliam, Mr. Fox, and other persons have property in the township.

This is a large and well built village, having two
manufactories of coarse linens, and its situation
seems well adapted to an extension of manufacturing
enterprise. There are two Springs, those of St.
Helen and St. Peter, which are said to be usefully
efficacious in certain complaints, but they are now
entirely neglected.

There is a Lectureship as well as a Curacy. The
latter is in the gift of the Vicar of Howden, the
former is in the rare patronage of the resident
householders. This diversity of patronage has, as
might be supposed, given rise to many disputes.

There are several extensive and useful Charities
in this township. In the reign of Edward Fourth,
Richard Garlthorpe left lands of considerable extent
to the Reading Minister, the poor, and other de-
serving objects. The funds of this bequest have
been impaired by the perversity of some of the
inhabitants, who contrived to get it into the Court
of Chancery. It is now free and unincumbered, and
is fairly and impartially administered by the present
Trustees.

In 1712, John Blanchard surrendered certain
lands in this place to trustees, for the benefit of a
Minister, whose duties and the mode of whose
election are pointed out in the surrender.   There
are other Charities, in addition to the above.

The Chapel, dedicated to St. Helen, stands
pleasantly upon an eminence and is said to have
been the tithe barn.   It is very neat, and has been
recently much improved, externally and internally,
to the great credit of the inhabitants.   There is a
good National School, Wesleyan, and other places
of worship.

There are two Ferries, one over the Ouse and
the other the Derwent.   A portion of this township
lies on the west side of the Derwent, where was
formerly the channel of this river.   This old channel
is now completely filled up, and the river has made
itself a new and more direct course to the Ouse.

There appears to have been forty owners of
lands here, and when they began to hold the open
fields in severalty, the several oxgangs so awarded
took the name of the several then owners, and so
continue.   This somewhat singular mode of desig-
nation gave rise to the frivolous and idle notion,
that William the Conqueror divided the township
amongst forty of his soldiers.

This village had long the reputation of being
the most litigious and quarrelsome in the neighbourhood.   In this respect it has recently much
improved.   The Rev. Thomas Guy, M.A. and Vicar
of Howden, resides here, and generally officiates.

VICARS OF THE PREBEND OF BARMBY.

1322. William de Skypwith, pres. by the P. and C. of Durham, m.
1337. Robert de Kelfield, cap. m.
1349. John Lenay, m.
1359. Henry de Birkenshaw, pbr. res. pro. Vic. de Wewyk.
1377. Robert Calthorp.
Rad. de Wirksop, pbr. m.
1394. William Blake, cap. m.
1412. Robert Dalby, pbr. m.
1427. William Laverack, pbr. m.
1466. John James, pbr. m.
1479. Robert Hadclyffe, res.
1480. Robert Johnson, als. Milner, m.
1510. Richard Stowe, m.
1528. Henry Holland. pbr. m.
1546. Christopher Ellis, pr. K. Hen. 8.

LECTURERS OF BARMBY.

The Rev. John Jackson, m.
1811. The Rev. Ralph Spofforth, M. A. m.
1824 The Rev. Thomas Guy, M. A.

INCUMBENTS OF BARMBY.

The Rev. John Mallison, m.
1793. The Rev. Robert Poole, m.
1843. The Rev. William Smith, res.
1846. The Rev. Henry Atkinson.

I

Balkholme

Is a small township with 165 inhabitants. Thomas Whitaker Esq. is the principal proprietor as also the owner of the mesne manor of Balkholme. It was formerly the property of the Metham family.

Belby,

A small township having 58 inhabitants. It is the property of I. C. Athorpe, Esq. of Dinnington.

Cotness

Contains 38 inhabitants and about 500 acres of land, it is principally the property of Philip Saltmarshe, Esq. and the Rev. Philip Simpson.

About the year 1770, Dr. Wells the medical adviser of the Duke of Kingston, had a small property here.

The house was tastefully built, with an ornamental garden around it. The well known Madam Latouche, then separated from the Duke to make way for his still better known and more notorious Duchess, resided in it. Her mysterious and sudden disappearance gave rise to much conjecture, it being supposed that she was kidnapped away for some secret purpose or other.

Kilpin

Contains 393 inhabitants and about 1000 acres of land, the property of I. C. Athorpe, Esq. the trus-

tees of the late Miss Mary Robinson, of Barlby, and
other proprietors. There is here a brick and tile
yard, a tannery establishment, and considerable river
traffic is carried on at Kilpin Pike, in this township.
The River Ouse forms its southern boundary.

Knedlington,

One mile west of Howden, anciently written Cledington. It contains 142 inhabitants and about 900 acres
of land. The tithes and ecclesiastical dues along with
those of Howden, constituted the first Prebend in
the Collegiate Church. This is a pleasant, well built
village, including the hamlet of Booth, and Barnhill-
hall. The latter was the residence of a branch of
the Metham family, in the time of Henry the
Seventh. It is now a farm house, and is moated
round.

At the west end of the village is the old hall,
formerly the property of a family named Arlush,
afterwards of the Weddells, Lords Grantham. Dr.
Samuel Terrick, at that time Chaplain of the Archbishop of York, married at Bishopthorpe in 1699,
Ann Arlush, widow. He enjoyed this property, in
her right, during life. He afterwards became
Bishop of London, and died in 1777.

The date of the building is not known, though
probably as early, if not earlier, than Elizabeth.
One room is panelled with oak, it contains some
good carving, with the arms of Terrick, Clarke, and
others. The building is a good specimen of early
domestic architecture, and is in a better state of pre-

servation than such buildings are commonly found to be in.

There is a Quakers' burial ground in the village, which has been disused as such for many years. Indeed, we are not aware that there is a single Quaker in the division of Howdenshire.

The residence of Thomas Clarke, Esq the owner of the manor, the ecclesiastical rights, and of nearly the whole of the township, is at the eastern end of the village.   It was built by Messrs. Weightman and Hadfield, in the years 1841 and 1842.   It is of strict Tudor character, with some stained glass by Warrington, of London.   The house stands in well wooded grounds, with pleasing views of the Churches of Howden and Goole, the River Ouse, and the surrounding country.   Many American trees, the seeds of which were imported into England by the late William Cobbet, were planted here, and they thrive very well.

The hamlet of Booth gives its name to the Ferry across the Ouse.   The ferry is the property of the Bishop of Ripon, and has long been leased to the Earl of Beverley.   This hamlet consisted but of one cottage for the ferryman, about the year 1600. The reader will regret to learn that the Booth Ferry Inn on the opposite side of the river is forthwith to be discontinued.   This has been for many years coupled with the name of Mr. William Wells, whose cordiality and liberality have doubtless often called to the memory of his guests the following well known lines,

"Whoe'er hath travel'd life's dull round,
    Whate'er his fortune may have been,
Will sigh to think how oft he found,
    His warmest welcome at an Inn."

Knedlington and the Arlush family gave the subject to an historical tale of the Civil Wars, published a few years ago, and entitled "Howden in the Month of April, 1644."

Laxton,

A Township and Chapelry, containing 266 inhabitants and 1500 acres of land, the property of various owners. There were formerly three manors in this Township, in the possession of the several families of Metham, Higdon, and Lowson. This with Skelton, formed the fourth Prebend in the Collegiate Church.

By an old terrier in possession of the Vicar, it appears that the Chapel of Laxton was given, granted, and erected, in the reign of Charles the First, by Ann Dorey, Elizabeth Dorey, and Grace Dorey, three maiden sisters. It has been improved in value by various donations, as well as by grants from Queen Anne's Bounty. This terrier was exhibited to the Archbishop at Hull, on his primary visitation in 1809. The vicarage is in the patronage of the Vicar of Howden.

VICARS OF THE PREBEND OF SKELTON AND LAXTON.

1330, Ds. Step. de Gribthorpe, pbr. pres. by the
 P. and C. of Durham, m.

1347. Alex. Bennet, pbr. m.

1349. William de Lynton, cap.

1380. Thomas Littester, pbr. res. pro. vic. de Wistow.

1402. John Green, pbr.
 Thomas Hill.

1445, Edm. Karr, cap.

1448. John Raynold, cap. m.

1462. John Watkinson, cap. m.

1476. John Ludwyn, pbr. m.

1501. John Gedling, pbr. res.

1508. Ds. Thomas Blacket, cap. m,

1521. R. Webster, preb. m.

1533. William Skelton, cap.
 Edward Richardson, m.

1537. Peter Batill, pbr. pres. by K. Hen. 8.

1540. Thomas Metingham.

After the Dissolution, the last Vicar had a pension
of five pounds annually, which he enjoyed in 1553.

INCUMBENTS SINCE THE ENDOWMENT OF THE CHAPEL.

John Mallinson, m.

1793. Robert Poole, m.

1843. William Smith, res.

1846. Philip Simpson, M.A. res.

1850. William Hutchinson, M.A.

Metham

Has 42 inhabitants, and about 900 acres of land, the property of the Rev. P. Simpson, and other proprietors. Mr. Simpson resides at the Hall, which is on the site, or nearly so, of the family mansion of the Methams.

Hugh Pudsey, Bishop of Durham, in the year 1154, granted to John Le Clerk of Howden, all the waste and marsh between Yuckflete and Cotnesse, unto the double ditch, which the said John caused to be made, bordering on lands of the men of Saltmarshe, which at this day is called the territory and manor of Metham. The first descendant of John Le Clerk, was Jordan de Metham, who assumed that name, and transmitted it to a wide spread family of successors, but the name is now extinct.

Two of them fell during the civil wars, fighting for Royalty. Sir Thomas Metham, Knt. was slain at Marston-moor, and Jordan his son, fell at Pomfret Castle. The family became greatly impoverished in the time of Sir George Metham, Knt. the last who bore the name. He sold the estate at Metham, and lived some years and died at North Cave, in the church of which place he lies buried.

Sir George appears to have been a most improvident person, and had little left to subsist upon, save a small annual pension from the crown. He rendered himself somewhat notorious by his connexion with the celebrated George Anne Bellamy, and is noticed in her autobiography.

The badge of the family was a fetterlock. In the year 1655, this badge carved in stone with the initials and date, " T. M. 1168," still remained in an old building near the hall. The annual payment or rent in fee, paid by John Le Clerk, is yet a charge upon the property and payable to the Bishop of Ripon.

Saltmarshe

Contains 157 inhabitants and about 900 acres of land. It is the property of Philip Saltmarshe, Esq. the Bishop of Ripon, and a few small proprietors. This family has long been resident and had property here, indeed it is most probable that they assumed their name from the place.

The late Philip Saltmarshe, Esq. built the hall, and greatly improved the village, which being well wooded, and the cottages luxuriantly covered with ivy and roses, presents a very pleasing object from the water. The view from the house is equally so, taking in a lake-like sweep of the river, with the distant Lincolnshire hills,

The Rev. John Saltmarshe, one of Cromwell's Chaplains, was of this family. He was a religious fanatic and a prolific author. His "Wonderful Prediction," and other works, are little known, except with the Huntingtonians and other extreme sects, however they yet retain their hold of public taste or individual fanaticism, in some parts of America.

He predicted the day and hour of his death to his wife and other persons, and he certainly died on the day he had fixed upon, as the account of his life and last moments quaintly says, "in the presence of many godly people of Quality."

He was often charged with betraying Sir John Hotham and his son, to the Parliament, and even the price of his treachery was named in some of the scurrilous pamphlets of the times. His power over the army appears to have been very considerable, and by consequence he was on intimate terms both with Fairfax and Cromwell.

Skelton

Contains 212 inhabitants, and upwards of 1500 acres of land. It is principally the property of William Scholfield, Esq. Philip Saltmarshe, Esq. the See of Ripon, T. H. S. Sotheron, Esq. and some smaller proprietors. Amongst these William Scholfield, Esq. is by far the largest, and his residence, Sand Hall, which is near the river, is surrounded by lands of the greatest richness and fertility.

Sir John Girlington, of a family near Richmond, was the owner of this property, which was sold by his widow, and by several intermediate conveyances this valuable estate became the property of the family of its present owner.

K

Thorpe,

A very small Township, contains fifty inhabitants, and two hundred and sixty acres of land. It is almost entirely the property of John Carver Athorpe, Esq.

Yokefleet

Contains two hundred and six inhabitants, and about one thousand acres of land, including allotments on Bishopsoil and Wallingfen. It is almost entirely the property of the Empson family. The river here is of considerable width and forms its southern boundary.

The Bishop of Durham occasionally claimed rights of fishing and other Manorial rights in the river, from Cawood to Melton, a distance of upwards of thirty miles. These exclusive rights, however, would hardly be found tenable at this day.

In the year 1342, two whales and two sturgeons were cast up on the shores of the Manor of Hoveden, which were carried away by the populace. As they were said to appertain to the Bishop of Durham, the King, Edward the Third, issued his writ to bring the offenders to justice. Thomas de Metham was at that time Seneschal of the Bishop, and the writ was directed to him amongst other persons.

In the year 1673 an order was made by the Mayor and Corporation of Hull for an enquiry into the fishgarths in the river, and a meeting was held at Howden. The visitors inspected the river, and they found two at Skelton, one at Sandhall Bank, two at Saltmarshe, and some others. These, they ordered to be pulled up and destroyed, and piles were driven down in various places, but so as not to endanger the navigation of the river.

The fisheries have during the last half century become nearly valueless, though formerly they were of considerable importance, nevertheless the productions of the river should not be overlooked. It cannot now be said to abound in Salmon, as it did some years ago, but what is taken, is not to be surpassed in flavour. Salmon Trout and Smelts are often plentiful. Many people now living remember vessels coming regularly from Holland, every year, up the river beyond Howden, to fish for Lampreys, which were taken in great quantities for bait. The Eels in the Derwent are considered particularly good.

If those persons who are immediately interested in the fisheries would exert themselves for the protection of the young fish, it seems pretty clear that the fisheries might again become productive and profitable. This remissness on their part is as unaccountable as it is inexcusable.

The parish of Howden being almost free from waste lands, and in general so well cultivated, it is not to be expected there should be found any great variety of wild flowers : and in so level a country we do not often meet with the rarer British Plants. It is not pretended here to give a Catalogue of the plants of the district, though it may be interesting to notice a few of them. In addition to the commonest plants which are found almost every where, on the warp land on the banks of the river may be seen in great profusion, the Meadow-saffron, the Rest-harrow, the Burnet, the Dewberry, the Arum or Wake-robin, the Melilot, the yellow Toadflax, the large blue Cranesbill, the Meadow-sweet, the clustered Campanula, the Lucerne, and other beautiful Vetches, the Valerian, and the Mugwort.

In the ditches and ponds there are the flowering Rush, the Frog-bit, the Water-soldier, the Arrow-head, the Buckbean, the pretty water Violet, the Bur-reed, the Catstail commonly called the Bullrush ; and on their margins, the yellow Iris, and several kinds of Willow-herb, and the Lythrum.

In the hedges, the black and white Bryony, the Nightshade, the Hop, and the large white Convolvulus, are found along with that handsome shrub the wild Guelder-rose, with its cheerful white flowers in the spring, and its bright scarlet berries and leaves in the autumn : only three Ferns, and they are of the commonest kinds, are met with in the lanes, and not more than three sorts of Orchis. The Twayblade, the Viper's Bugloss, the Loose-strife, the wild Teazle, and Henbane, grow in a few situations ; but perhaps all the plants mentioned yield in interest to the few with which all associate pleasant thoughts and happy hours, the Rose, the Honeysuckle, the Violet, the Cowslip, and the early Primrose.

In noticing the Natural History of the neighbourhood, in however cursory a way, it would not do to omit the immense number of birds, every spring apparently on the increase, which make the air vocal with their music. A complete list of the birds would include a much greater variety of species than is generally supposed to be observed in a country of so tame a character, though the kinds are not so numerous, particularly of birds of passage, as in the south of England. The White-throat, a species of Nightingale, sings nearly all night, great part of the spring and summer ; Thrushes and Blackbirds abound, the gray and golden Plover, the Jay, the Heron, the Corncrake, the Wild duck, two varieties of the Snipe, the Woodcock, the Hawk, the Bunting, the Kingfisher, the Hooded-crow, the Cuckoo, are among the less frequent kinds. Of Fieldfares, Wagtails, Swallows, Martins, Yellow-hammers, Robin Redbreasts, &c. there seems to be no end. However little these tenants of the hedge rows, furrows, trees, and eaves of houses, may be valued where they are so plentiful, it is scarcely possible to conceive the blank their disappearance would create, and how dreary is the contrast in those parts of the country where there is little wood, and few birds, to attract either the eye or the ear.

Nor should the Skylark be forgotten, which "Up to Heaven's gate sings," a bird which has given rise to so many poetic effusions, none of them surpassing in beauty the exquisite lines of the Ettrick Shepherd.

The Skylark.

Bird of the wilderness,
Blythesome and cumberless,
Sweet be thy matin o'er moorland and lea!
Emblem of happiness,
Blest is thy dwelling place,
O to abide in the desert with thee;
Wild is thy lay and loud,
Far in the downy cloud,
Love gives it energy, love gave it birth,
Where on thy dewy wing
Where art thou journeying?
Thy lay is in heaven, thy love is on earth.

O'er fell and fountain sheen,
O'er moor and mountain green,
O'er the red streamer that heralds the day,
Over the cloudlet dim,
Over the rainbow's rim,
Musical cherub, soar, singing, away;
Then, when the gloaming comes,
Low in the heather blooms,
Sweet will thy welcome and bed of love be;
Emblem of happiness,
Blest is thy dwelling place—
O to abide in the desert with thee!

HOGG.

The river Derwent, which partly forms the western boundary of the Manor, was made navigable by an Act of Parliament passed in the first year of the reign of Queen Anne. The original contractors and the owners of the tolls, sold them to the Marquis of Rockingham, from whom they passed to their present owner, Earl Fitzwilliam.

The prevaling disease of the district is Dyspepsia, and such complaints as result therefrom, but on the whole it may be considered very healthy, more especially so, if the existence of many persons of an advanced age may be offered as a proof of its ordinary salubrity. However, it behoves all persons, as far as they can, to attend to the improvement of the Drainage, recently much neglected.

In the year 1726, an act was obtained for improving the navigation of the river Ouse. The Lord Mayor and Corporation of York were made Trustees, and a numerous body of landed proprietors were made Commissioners for carrying the provisions of the Act into effect. This, like many other projects of a similar kind, produced no adequate result.

Amongst other powers given, was that of deepening and straightening the course of the river, and it was projected to cut off the peninsula in Skelton, by a direct cut from that village to Saltmarshe. Had this been done the Port of Goole never would have been made, and the face of the country would have been widely different from what it is at present.

The drainage of the country is now in such a state,

if an Act of Parliament cannot be obtained to improve it, most assuredly the Court of Sewers should be revived and recommissioned.   Whoever opposes both of these very desirable measures, must be set down as an injurer of the general health, and an enemy of the poor and helpless, whom ignorance and penury always place in the van of those who fall the victims of damp, noisomeness, and malaria.

The drainage of the neighbourhood is certainly worse than it was some years ago, arising from the discontinuance of the Court of Sewers, and it is to be feared it will become still worse, unless some active and immediate steps are taken to stay the downward progress.

The agricultural labourers of the district are skilful, powerful, and active, well fitted for and acquainted with the humble duties they are called upon to perform.   They are for the most part exemplary, honest, and industrious, and imbued with feelings of self-respect and independence.   The rewards given by the Agricultural Society and the occasional investigations of the Board of Guardians, have often brought to light traits of integrity, kindness, and right heartedness, which do honour to our common nature.

As to agricultural servants, male and female, they are not on a par with the labourers.   It is unfortunate for them that they are rarely called upon to produce a certificate of character from their last employer.   If every farmer at the time of hiring would insist upon this, he himself would be much better served, and what is of greater importance, the civility, regularity, and moral habits of the servants, could not fail to be improved by its adoption.

The district has for a very long time been free from crimes of a dark dye. It is peaceable, orderly, and possibly, considerably above an average, on the score of honesty. There has been but one incendiary fire, and even that might be traced to feelings smarting under the impulse of fancied insult and oppression.

Village Book-Clubs might be established with great advantage, especially if confined to books of a practical and useful kind. They would have a tendency to keep the labourers from the public houses, which are too numerous, and often prove incentives too powerful for the poor man to resist, especially where his own fireside is not cheered by those humble, English comforts, and by that smile of alacrity and love, ever the best restoratives for a wearied and o'erlaboured frame.

Village Flower Shows and Vegetable Exhibitions, would be of use, with trifling rewards to the successful candidates. The rules and regulations of "The Pytchley Horticultural Society," drawn up by The Rev. Abner Brown, and published by Wertheim & Mackintosh, London, price two-pence, may be easily procured, and are as good and simple as any which can be adopted. Such competition could not fail to add to the cottager's comfort and happiness. A Village Cow-Club may be named as

L

another useful rural institution. Nothing, indeed, can come amiss which teaches the mind to rely upon itself, which wards off or lightens the oppressive feelings of poverty and dependence, and which makes the poor man proudly conscious that he is a link in that chain which binds together an enterprizing, an independent, and a prosperous Nation.

It would appear from the following letter, dated in the year 1475, that even before the Reformation, no small difficulty was found in collecting the old and customary payments of Howdenshire. Dane-gelt and Peter-pence were at all times obnoxious exactions, and often productive of vexation and strife. It is to be presumed that a very small portion of the pence thus raised found its way into the coffers of the Pope, nevertheless stringent orders were often sent from Rome to urge on and insist upon its collection in every part of the Kingdom.

"Litera directa domino Thomœ Metham et magistro Saltmerssh,

Right honorable and worshipfull srez, I commend me unto you thanking you hertfully of ye grete zele, luff, and favour, ye which ye have evermore born unto yat gloriouse confessor Saynt Cuthbert and his poor monastery of Duresme, beseking you alway of good continuannce. And for somuch as I am informed yat yer are certayn persones dwelling within Hoveden and Hovedenshir wher I stand ordinary and have ordinary Jurisdiccion, ye which are obstinate against ye kirk and will noght pay unto my officers ne unto ye curate Rome penys as other men wele disposid have don. Wherof I and my predecessours have ben peaseably possessed fro tyme of mynde, but manysshih thaim and thretith thaim. Insomuch yat yai dare never aske ye said Romepenys ne exercise my Jurisdiccion in dew forme as yai shuld for doute of ye lifes withoute better supportacion : of you and othir gentilmen of ye cuntry like as maistre William Laybron, myn official of ye forsaid jurisdiccion can informe you more largly. Wherefor aftir a consideracion herof I beseke you hertfully to stand good and tendre maistres unto my said officers and curats of ye said Jurisdiccion, mayntenyng and supporting yaim after conscience and right noght only in askyng, gedering, receyveing, and perservyng of ye said Rome penys the which are dew, but also kepyng of my jurisdiccion at ye reverence of God and of Saynt Cuthbert. And as I and my brethir may be your continuell bedemen during our lifes. Writyn at Duresme, &c."

In the month of December, 1850, the most numerous and most enthusiastic Meeting ever held in Howden, assembled to condemn the aggression of the Pope, and the insult offered by him to this Kingdom. Hardly was there absent from it a respectable and right thinking man of the town or neighbourhood, all equally and alike aroused to a sense of the outrage offered by a powerless and deluded Pope, to a powerful, free, and indignant people.

At that very time there was rapidly rising from the ground, a large Roman Catholic Chapel—to woo, to win, or to cajole the inhabitants from the worship of their forefathers, to invite them to become Renegades to their Religion and Traitors to their Faith. If the spirit, the energy, the unanimity, and the determination of that Meeting were a reality, and not an empty show, not one apostate inhabitant of the Town of Howden will ever plant his foot within its walls.

As sure as he does so—as assuredly will he surrender his mental independence — as assuredly will he introduce distrust and misery into the bosom of his family—and as assuredly, sooner or later, will he lend a helping hand to sap and undermine the hard-won liberties of his native Land. While, however, the enthusiastic cheers of that Meeting still ring in our ears, we have no fear that the Sons of those who gave utterance to them will be able to say of their Sires — " They were apostates from their Faith — They entailed upon us the misery and the slavery under which we groan."

The following Letter from an unknown pen, recently appeared in the Public Newspapers and Reviews, on a subject of the warmest interest to the inhabitants of Howden.

"To the Rev. Thomas Guy, M. A. Vicar of Howden.

Reverend Sir,

In common with many other persons I have very often contemplated with pleasure the great and laudable improvements made in the Church of Howden, by yourself, your churchwardens, and the parishioners. They have been so great as to elicit general applause—so liberal as to command admiration—and so tastefully carried out as to meet the approval of all. These labours, now continued for a series of years, are nearly brought to a successful termination, and the beautiful fabric stands forth and challenges the criticism of the most captious observer, as it equally does the love and veneration of every one of your parishioners.

Would there had been no one to mar your work —and above all, would the blow had not been struck by the Bishop of Ripon.

The Prebendal Residences, forming the eastern boundary of the churchyard, were erected about four hundred years ago, and they might easily have stood four hundred more. They survived the Reformation, they passed unscathed through destructive civil broils, yet are they doomed to fall, in the year 1850, by a hand more ruthless than both. No one can witness the demolition of this interesting building without pain, and all alike are equally loud in the expression of their astonishment and sorrow.

For a long series of years they were the residences of the Prebendaries of the Collegiate Church, many of them alike illustrious for the position they maintained in their lives, and equally honourable in the transmitted and enduring memorials of their usefulness and sanctity. Again, under these almost historic walls, and around these now-demolished buildings, annually assembled, from every part of Europe, that multitude of traffickers of every kind and description, in whose hands were the trade and commerce of the middle ages, and who sought the shadow of this holy precinct for the protection of their goods and merchandise. Leipsic, and a few other places, yet present similar gatherings, which may be looked upon as the foundation of a commerce which now overshadows the world. But neither the reminiscences of their sanctity—their interest as illustrating the manners and customs of a bygone age—neither the love of past generations, nor the veneration of the present, could stay the hand of the destroyer. The materials, for which they have been unroofed, tumbled down, and their very foundations dug up—may be worth forty pounds.

In the year 1267, a portion of the cemetery yard was set apart whereon to erect these prebendal residences. So says the order for their endowment. At the dissolution of the Collegiate Church the prebendal property vested in the crown, and was by the crown granted in fee to several grantees, to hold as fully, entirely, and subject to the self-same rights and privileges, as the prebendaries had heretofore held it. This property, then, clearly passed by this grant to the grantees, or, if not, it must have reverted to the parish, as an inalienable portion of the churchyard. The bishops were at no period, and in no way, parties to this endowment, nor did they participate in any grant from the crown.

Let us hope, then, that this time-honoured monument of other days will be restored, the wanton destruction of which has equally outraged the feelings of the stranger and the inhabitant. You and your parishioners, at great pains and expence, have laboured twenty years to preserve and restore the beauty and characteristic architecture of one of the most interesting places in England, while three days wanton desecration have more than undone all your labours—aye, and illegally undone them. Let me beg of you to enter the churchyard, and painfully judge for yourself; and would you know the grateful feelings of the inhabitants of Howden towards the Lord of the Manor—*circumspice.*

> I am, Reverend Sir,
>
> Your obedient Servant,
>
> MŒSTUS."

In a few years hardly a trace will remain of these most interesting buildings, nay, their very site will soon be unknown, after an existence of six hundred years. Now, who can wend his way along a path so recently hallowed by such old and endeared reminiscences, without the sense of such a wanton bereavement. Every feeling has been outraged, every youthful and endeared association has been rooted up, the antique character of an old and respectable Town has been as wantonly as barbarously destroyed, and the answer to its reasonable and feeling prayer, has been silence, mockery, and insult.

The person in whose name this wrong has been done, is an Antiquarian, a Scholar, and a Gentleman, and could he see the effect of a too easy compliance with the representations of others, or could he know the pain he has inflicted, we are assured he would most deeply regret this wanton desecration. But filling the exalted situation he does, this offers no excuse for even passively tolerating an act, disgraceful alike to every one connected with it. In the Heads of the Church, we look for, and we have a right to find, protectors not despoilers, of the ancient monuments of piety and veneration which adorn our Land. It is their duty to see with their own eyes, and deferentially to consider the feelings of the public, and not to leave that public to the Vandalism of their dependants.

Let us hope that there is somewhere a Power yet in existence to which we may appeal, and let us hope that our appeal will not be made in vain,

" Tandem resurge, et hostium superbiam
Compesce : perde funditùs
Hostes protervos, qui tuum sacrarium
Manu nefandâ polluunt."

THE END.

W. F. Pratt, Printer. Howden.

L' Envoye.

On the lone Moor, alike remote
    From human joy and care—
Thy faithful spirit fans my cheek,
    And tells me Thou art there.

O'er the wide Sea when darkness rests,
    Or evening's golden glare—
Thy watchful spirit murmuring low,
    Assures me Thou art there.

When the pale Moon stoops from her cloud,
    Mov'd by a lover's prayer—
Her sweet beam like thy sweeter eyes,
    Points to Thy spirit there.

In smiles, in tears—by day, by night—
    Mid danger and despair—
In heaven, on earth—in life, in death—
    Thou wilt be ever there.